Gearhead Garage

STOCK CARS

LUKE COLINS

BLACK
RABBIT
BOOKS

Bolt is published by Black Rabbit Books
P.O. Box 3263, Mankato, Minnesota, 56002.
www.blackrabbitbooks.com
Copyright © 2017 Black Rabbit Books

Design and Production by Michael Sellner
Photo Research by Rhonda Milbrett

Library of Congress Control Number: 2015954680

HC ISBN: 978-1-68072-035-8   PB ISBN: 978-1-68072-262-8

Printed in the United States at CG Book Printers,
North Mankato, Minnesota, 56003. PO #1790 4/16

Web addresses included in this book were working and appropriate
at the time of publication. The publisher is not responsible for broken
or changed links.

Image Credits

Dreamstime: Walter Arce,
Back Cover, 1, 4–5, 14 (tires); Welco-
mia, 15 (brakes); Flickr: 11; Shutterstock:
abrakadabra, 7, 10, 28–29 (car); Action Sports
Photography, 3, 6–7,13, 23, 32; apiguide, 25;
Castleski, 28; Daniel Huerlimann-BEELDE, 16–17;
Doug James, Cover, 18, 20–21, 26; Everett Collec-
tion, 8; Ken Tannenbaum, 29 (towers); Matthew
Jacques, 31; Renewer, 15 (radiator); Rudy Balasko,
15 (transmission); Steve Bower, 14, 18–19 (engine);
Wikipedia: Darryl Moran, 29 (Earnhardt)
Every effort has been made to contact copyright
holders for material reproduced in this book.
Any omissions will be rectified in subse-
quent printings if notice is given to
the publisher.

CONTENTS

CHAPTER 1

Front of the Pack

Rows of stock cars follow the
pace car around the track. Drivers
weave, testing their steering. The green
flag waves. The cars roar off.

One car takes a quick lead.
But cars in back slowly sneak up.
Drivers fight for the lead. That's
where everyone wants to be when
the race ends.

Popular Sport

Stock car racing is one of the most popular sports in the United States. Cars race around oval tracks. They reach speeds above 200 miles (322 kilometers) per hour. These cars are built for speed. They are also built to keep drivers safe.

Where Stock Car Racing Is Popular

Canada   Brazil   Australia
United States   Argentina   New Zealand
Mexico   United Kingdom

CHAPTER 2

The History of Stock Cars

Stock cars look a bit like cars people drive every day. And there's a reason for that. The first stock cars were people's everyday cars!

In the 1920s, people wanted to make their cars faster. They made changes to the **engines**. Some of these cars went 120 miles (193 km) per hour. Soon, drivers started racing their fast cars. Stock car racing was born.

Organizing the Sport

Interest in stock cars continued to grow. People began to organize races. They created rules too. These rules told drivers what they could do to their cars.

In the early days, racers could change their cars only a little.

Stock Cars Today

Over the years, the organizations changed their rules. Drivers still use cars that look similar to everyday cars. But they are changed quite a lot. They use more powerful engines. They're also designed for good air flow.

Companies know many fans watch stock car races. They pay to have their logos painted on the cars.

By the Numbers

Pro teams spend about $400,000 EVERY WEEK. Here's how some of that money is spent.

$100,000 ON ENGINES

$32,000 ON TIRES

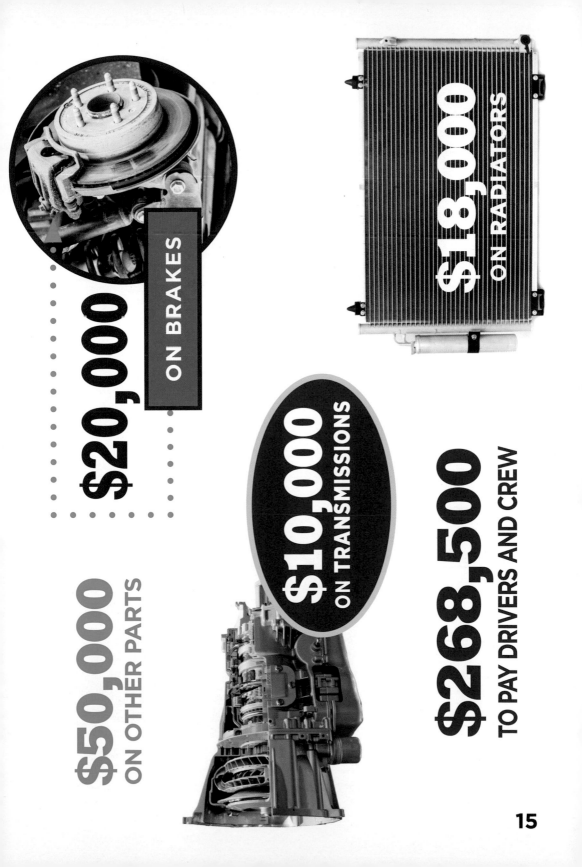

$20,000 ON BRAKES

$18,000 ON RADIATORS

$10,000 ON TRANSMISSIONS

$50,000 ON OTHER PARTS

$268,500 TO PAY DRIVERS AND CREW

CHAPTER 3

Built

for Speed

Stock car bodies are built for speed. The **nosepiece** is low. This position directs air over the car. The wheel openings stick out from the tires. This design pushes air away from the car.

77 inches wide
(196 centimeters)

Weighs
**3,300
pounds**
(1,497 kilograms)

**196.2
inches long**
(498 centimeters)

Stock Car Engines

Stock cars use V-8 engines to get the speed fans love. An engine's temperature can reach 2,000 degrees Fahrenheit (1,093 degrees Celsius). So these engines are built thicker and stronger than everyday engines.

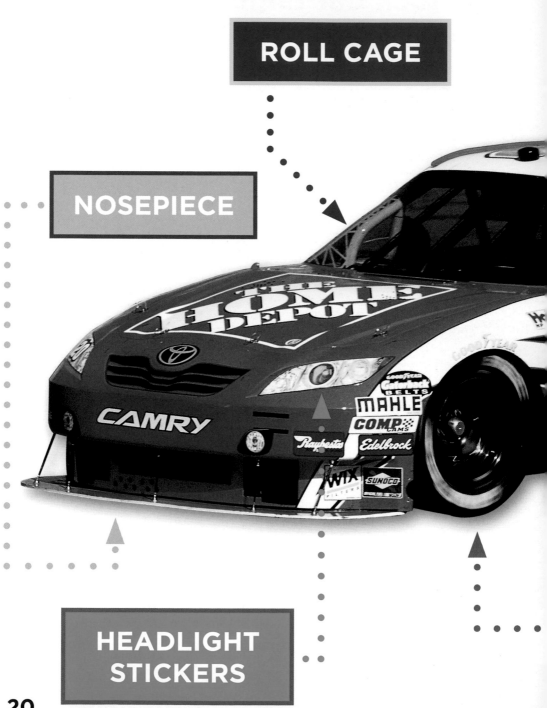

ROLL CAGE

NOSEPIECE

HEADLIGHT STICKERS

REAR SPOILER

WINDOW NET

HOME DEPOT #2829

20

TIRES

Safety Features

Racing at high speeds is dangerous. Stock cars have safety features that protect drivers. Seats wrap around drivers' ribs and shoulders. This design supports drivers during a crash.

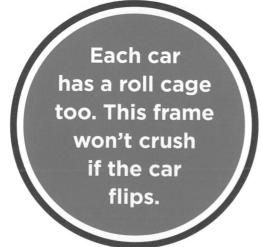

Each car has a roll cage too. This frame won't crush if the car flips.

CHAPTER 4

The Future of Stock Cars

Teams are always trying to make faster and safer cars. New technology will play a role in future stock cars. Maybe new fuels will power stock cars. Or maybe 3D printing will help create new parts.

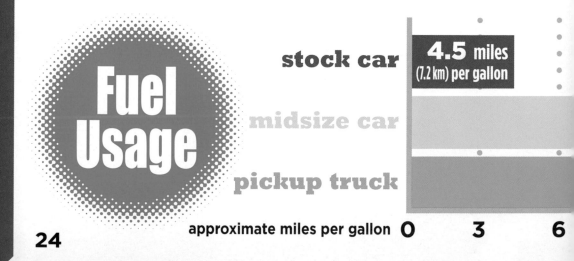

Fuel Usage

stock car — **4.5** miles (7.2 km) per gallon

midsize car

pickup truck

approximate miles per gallon 0   3   6

25 miles
(40 km) per gallon

19 miles
(30.6 km) per gallon

9   12   15   18   21   24   27

Roaring On

No one knows what future stock cars will look like. But one thing's for sure. Fans love the roar and speed of these cars. Future stock cars are sure to be

fun to watch.

1947

National Association for Stock Car Racing (NASCAR) starts.

1979

First stock car race is shown on TV.

1945

World War II ends.

1945

The first people walk on the moon.

1969

2001

Racer Dale Earnhardt Sr. dies in a crash. Stock cars get many safety features following this disaster.

2013

NASCAR uses the Generation-6 cars that look more like everyday cars.

2016

Terrorists attack the World Trade Center and Pentagon.

2001

engine (EN-jin)—a machine that changes energy into mechanical motion

nosepiece (NOZ-pees)—the bottom area of a car under the hood

pace car (PAYS KAR)—an automobile that leads race cars through a lap before a race

radiator (RAY-de-ay-tuhr)—a device used to keep the engine of a vehicle from getting too hot

transmission (tranz-MI-shun)—a group of parts that takes energy from the engine to an axle that moves

weave (WEEV)—to move in a zigzag motion

BOOKS

David, Jack. *Stock Cars.* Cool Rides. Minneapolis: Bellwether Media, 2008.

Mason, Paul. *Stock Cars.* Motorsports. Mankato, MN: Amicus, 2011.

Riggs, Kate. *Stock Cars.* Seedlings. Mankato, MN: Creative Education, 2014.

WEBSITES

About NASCAR
www.nascar.com/en_us/news-media/articles/about-nascar.html

NASCAR Fast Facts
www.cnn.com/2013/09/06/us/nascar-fast-facts/

NASCAR Stock Cars
www.sciencechannel.com/tv-shows/how-its-made/videos/how-its-made-nascar-stock-cars/

INDEX

C

costs, 14–15

E

engines, 9, 12, 19

F

fuel, 24–25

H

history, 9, 10, 12, 28–29

N

nosepieces, 16, 20

R

roll cages, 20, 22

S

safety, 6, 22, 29

sizes, 16–17

speeds, 6, 9, 19, 27

T

tires, 20–21

tracks, 4, 6